From Midgard to Hel - A Heathens Journey After Death

First Edition

B.D.France

From Midgard to Hel

For my family with love

"If you don't find me in Asgard you'll find me in Hel" - B.D.France

This book is part of a collection of work by Ben Desmond France from the book "All from a dream..."

For more work and information on Ben Desmond France visit www.facebook.com/BDFranceBooks or find my books on Amazon.

From Midgard to Hel

Content

Acknowledgements.. i

Introduction.. 1

Norse mythology- The beginning............... 3

Part one- Introduction to Hel..................... 7

Part two- The Realm of Hel...................... 11

Part three- The journey to Hel................. 15

Part four- The Goddess Hel...................... 19

Part five- Burials and traditions............. 25

Part six- My final words
        & acknowledgement................... 31

Extra information & useful links............. 35

From Midgard to Hel

Acknowledgements

A special thank you to my son Jake Howell and wife Leanne for helping with the editing of this book.

A huge thank you to my wife and children for their patients while I have been working on this book. I Love you xxx

A special thank you to Nick Wouters for his input on Volva's and other information.

A huge thank you to Gareth Hockin for your endless help and guidance since day one with some of the content and introduction.

A thank you to Asatru UK. Kin, Moderators and members for inspiring me to do this book.

And a huge Thank you Woden Thing kindred for all there support

From Midgard to Hel

Picture By Ben Desmond France 2019

Introduction

This book is based on a oral tradition which developed over thousands of years, sadly much of this has been lost to the sands of time either through loss of culture or deliberate destruction of traditions. What I hope to do through this work is to recreate the spirit of that tradition using what I have learned through personal study and my own imagination, I make no claims for historical authenticity in this book, I'm writing this book as a easy read overview of death and the afterlife in Hel in the heathen belief.

Norse mythology the beginning

In the beginning of time, there was a void called Ginnungagap. To the south was Muspell a place bright and full of flames and to the north a freezing land called Niflheim. In the midst of Niflheim was a spring called Hvergelmir from that spring ran eleven rivers. As the rivers ran from the source, the poisonous lees that they deposited began to harden into ice. When the ice stopped hardening the vapour from the poison froze into frost layers across Ginnungagap. In the south there was sparks and hot winds coming from Muspell.

As the heat and frost met the moisture from the melting ice began life. From those droplets formed the giant Ymir who gave rise to a race of frost giants. From Ymir's sweat from his left armpit Ymir grew a male and female, while one of his legs begot a giant son. Further ice melted and created Audhumla the cow whose udders flowed rivers of milk for Ymir. Audhumla licked salty rime stones and after three days emerged a complete man called Buri he then had a son called Bor who married Bestla the daughter of the frost giant Bolthorn. Together they had three sons Odin, Vili and Ve who in time decided to kill Ymir. Soon after Ymirs death there was so much blood the race of frost giants drowned and only Bergelmir escaped to later become the leader of the new giant race and from Ymir's body Odin created Midgard. The three brothers came upon two tree trunks and created a man and a woman who they named Ask (ash tree) and Embla (elm tree) the three brothers Odin, Vili

and VE then gave Ask and Embla breath and life.
From this first couple came and from them all who
lived in Midgard.

Not long after these events more gods, race's and
realms began to appear and a great war would rage
between two groups of gods, known as The Aesir
and The Vanir. After a long fight and a exchange of
members the war had finally ended and both sides
realised they were equal. As peace was restored the
two groups of gods went their own ways, the Aesir
to Asgard and the Vanir to Vanaheimr. Just after
the war Loki's partner Angrboda gave birth to three
children one of which was the Goddess Hel. The
gods feared her and Odin banished her to the only
realm that was un ruled and that was Helheim.
from Helheim she ruled over the dead that died of
sickness and old age. Odin and Freya (Freya is the
goddess who gets first choice of half of the dead
who die in battle) are the God's who collect the
fallen warriors from the battlefield to take them to
Asgard for their own.

From Midgard to Hel

Part one
Introduction to Hel

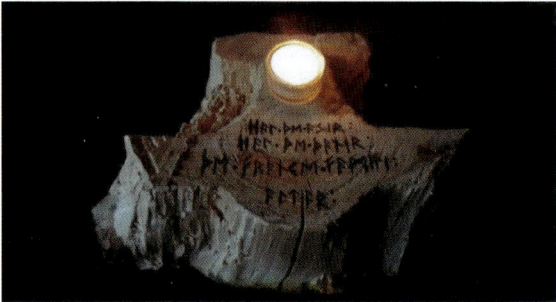

Picture By Ben Desmond France 2019

As the pagan religion of Heathenry slowly began to disappear as Christianity began to take over in Western Europe. It is possible Hel now known as "hell" by the Christian belief would be a place where sinners or non Christians would go and be trapped there forever for their sins as a punishment. As the idea of a Christian heaven grew more popular and more appealing to the people of Europe, dying a warrior's death and going to Valhalla (Odin's Hall), Folkvang (Freya's Hall) or even Hel the peaceful afterlife of Heaven grew more popular as the years went by.

To this day not much is known about Hel, what we do know is what has been found in the sagas or eddas of old Norse mythology. Death like in many different beliefs is a journey of the spirit to its final destination. In different beliefs the destinations can vary extremely from places of pure paradise or peacefulness to places of extreme torture and pain and this is where Hel is different.

In the most common stories told of Hel, it is a place where only people who have died of sickness or old age may enter. It is a place where life seems to go on as if the spirit does not know its dead. Continuing his/her every day activities and reuniting with ancestors who passed from life before them. In some sources I have read they say some of the dead who go to Hel are welcomed as honoured guests to a table of fine food and mead .

So how does one begin on the path to Hel? Once the soul leaves the body and what happens? and how do you get to the path or road? These questions I've looked into many times and only found other people's points of view with no specific confirmation of facts.

My view is that when the soul leaves the body you awake standing on a path and all around you is covered in thick grey fog. you have no idea your dead or feel fear of being dead just the feeling of calmness or peacefulness. From out of the fog an ancestor approaches, someone you had strong connections in life with and he/she will meet you carrying a lantern and guide you along the path over Gjallarbrú (the bridge) into Hel.

This is how I see the soul move's on after death and how each soul begins its journey to its final place and maybe the light that you see as you begin to pass is the glow of the lantern in the thick grey fog .

From Midgard to Hel

**Part two
The Realm of Hel**

Picture By Ben Desmond France 2019

Hel is described in some books as being a mountainous place that is cold, dark, damp and covered in fog.   A place where the sun is always down or at dusk when visited by a living person. In the story of Baldur's death when Hermod visits Hel he stays the night until morning. This also means Hel has a day and night cycle like the other worlds, but to view Hel by someone who is dead the place appears similar to life in Midgard (living earth) a land similar to the one they had left behind or better.

Hel's location in the Norse cosmos varies in different books some say that Hel is found in a region of Niflheim and in other books it says that Hel, also known as Helheim, is a Realm of its own. Hel is always said to be found down and north, it is possible that it could be located in a valley and that it can be seen from some places in Midgard.

On the border of Hel runs the river Gjöll that originates from the wellspring Hvergelmir in Niflheim, flowing through Ginnungagap. Gjöll is the river that flows closest to the gate of the underworld with the bridge Gjallarbrú that goes over it which leads into the land of the dead. Located somewhere between Niflheim and Hel lives the dragon called Níðhöggr who gnaws at a roots of the world tree known as Yggdrasil. In some books it is said that the dragon sucks the blood out of the newly dead on arrival. There is also a farm of an unnamed giantess located somewhere on the path to Hel.

 Between Hel and Midgard, possibly closer to Hel, is a mythical cave called Gnipahellir (Gnipa cave) which translates into English as cliff cave. It is said that from the cave it is possible to see Nagrindr (Hell Gate) or gates of Hel. This gives a small bit of evidence that Hel is located below the other realms. This cave is also home to Garmr, the hellhound who guards the gates of Hel, in some stories Garmr is also described as bound like Fenrir. This may explain why some heathens think the two wolves may be the same. However Garmr fights a different battle during Ragnarok, which would seem to make them two different wolves.

The cave may also have some possible connection with the story of Loki being bound. In the story Loki is chained to three rocks in an unknown cave. This is where a snake is hung above him slowly dripping venom onto his face until the day Ragnarök comes. Loki was placed in the cave as punishment for tricking the blind god Hod into killing Baldur with a branch of mistletoe. Loki's wife Sigyn stands beside him with a bowl catching some of the venom until the bowl is full. When she moves to empty the bowl it is said that the venom that drops on Loki causes him to writhe so violently he causes earthquakes.

Part three
The journey to Hel

Picture By Ben Desmond France 2019

In different books and stories I have read about the journey to the gates of Hel, a lot of them are similar in ways describing the journey there. One of the stories that tell of the journey is "The Death Of Baldur". Hermod (the son of the god Odin) travels to Hel to offer a ransom to the Goddess Hel for Baldur's release.

From Asgard it took Hermod nine nights riding Odin's horse (Sleipnir, another child of Loki) through dark, deep, cold valleys along Hel's Road. The road to Hel (the place) is called Helvegr and it eventually reaches the river Gjoll. It is written in some books that the river as it flows is said to sound like a furious battle like steel clashing upon a battlefield, in other books is said to sound like souls yelling in pain. To cross over into Hel there is a bridge called Gjallarbrú which is over the river Gjoll.

In some of the stories I have read, the bridge is described as having a thatched roof made of solid gold but the wood of the structure is worn and beaten by the river. At the entrance to the bridge stands a guardian called Móðguðr who is briefly described in some books as a young woman. She allows the newly dead to cross from one side to the other and often asks for a name along with a reason for crossing. Móðguðr stands guard to make sure the dead do not cross back over again back into the land of the living.

When Hermod was allowed to cross the bridge Móðguðr told Hermod that Hel could be found down and north. She also said that days before his arrival that a army had crossed the bridge into Hel. This means that Hel could also be a default destination for the dead. Hermod was informed by her that Baldur had also recently crossed the Bridge riding a horse (This may suggest that whatever you're buried with or cremated with you, you take with you to the other side).

Continuing along the road to the other side of the bridge the path begins to descend north into what seems to be a valley, it's possible that along this path is the Ironwood which is a forest with iron-leafed trees . The mythical cave called Gnipahellir (Gnipa cave, cliff cave) is possibly located on this path. In the cave lives a chained up wolf who is called Garmr, the hellhound who guards the gates of Hel, this may also mean that it's not a long path to walk to reach the gates or wall of Hel from the bridge.

The wall of Hel referred to as several names like Helgrindr, The Fence of Hel, Nágrindr, Corpse-Fence, Valgrindr, The Fence of the Fallen. I imagine from what I have seen in other literature is for it to be so tall that no one can climb over the walls and it would be made of stone or wood with defences . I also imagine the gates to be made of wood or iron with gold guiding and one of the roots of Yggdrasil growing over the top of the whole structure and for Hel's home to resemble a fortress.

Part four
The Goddess Hel and her home

Picture By Ben Desmond France 2019

I imagine Hel (Place) on the inside to look like an old fortress with tall wood or stone walls all around and a long house made of stone in the centre, with one of Yggdrasil roots grown over it. I imagine there are small houses made of wood that surround it like a village and all the streets are lit by candle lit lanterns. In the centre of the fort I imagine Hel's Hall (the stone long house) to appear to be crumbling from the length of time standing, with a roof made of wood or thatch.

Inside Hel's Hall I imagine it to look totally different, the hall to have a stone floor covered in straw for comfort. Wooden walls covering the old stone and decorated with displays of hunted animal

furs and valuable weapons. In one corner of the
main hall is a large spit that roasts a whole animal
to feed the welcomed guests of the Goddess Hel.
The guests would sit at a large, long, dark wooden
table with jugs full of the finest mead. Finally at the
other end of the table are two thrones, one made of
stone with a bears skin over it and this would be the
seat for the Goddess Hel and the other made of
wood with gold guiding and this would be the
honoured seat for the god Baldur. Decorated
corridors that lead to bedrooms where the beds are
filled with straw and have fur blankets covering
them and all of the rooms and corridors would be lit
by candle light.

It was said that the great hall of Hel was called
Elvidner ("misery"). It was said that her dish or
Bowl was called Hunger with her knife called
Greed or famine. Her partner or husband was called
Idleness and her maid was called Sloth. Her other
belongings were also named with bed being called
Sorrow, her threshold was called ruin and curtains
were called Conflagration.

Hel also had a horse that went by the name of
Helhest, Helhest was a three legged horse that
roamed Hel (the place) until Hel (the Goddess)
needed its service to ride to Midgard to collect a
dead soul or souls. Helhest is associated with death
and illness and is often mentioned in some Danish
folklore and has been seen often to be wondering
graveyards at night. According to some documented

information, Helhest is a ghost from a sacrifice of a burial grave, the horse had its leg cut off to stop it from running away .

The Goddess/Giantess Hel is known as Queen of the underworld. She is the daughter of the trickster God Loki and the Giantess Sorceress Angrboda. Her siblings were Jormungandr the Midgard serpent and Fenrir the wolf. In some books it says that the children were born in a dark cave in Jotunheim and the gods saw them as symbols of pain, sin, and death. The Aesir God's feared Loki's three children so they bound Fenrir, cast Jormugandr into the sea and banished Hel to the underworld and from this began Hel's rule in Helheim (Hel). Odin then granted Hel rule over the Nine Worlds and it's dead.

Hel is said to be a Gentle kind hearted goddess who welcomes each person to her realm. On appearance she is split down the centre of her body. Half a beautiful woman with fair skin, blond hair and beautiful eyes and the other half of the skin Blue, pale or even as bone. In other descriptions she appears as a old woman. Hel is commonly described as wearing a grey/ black worn Hooded cloak or Long dress and she's sometimes is holding a staff.

Hel appears in a few of the stories of the gods.   In one of the stories Loki takes the God Thor to the land of the giants and Thor is set three challenges by the giants one of which was to beat a old, Frail woman in combat. Thor after many of attempts of trying to defeat the woman finally admits he cannot win. Thor known for his strength and capability could never win this fight because the old, frail woman was the Goddess Hel in disguise. The Giant told Thor that there was no way he could beat the old woman because you cannot beat death, death always wins.

Some mythological stories that Hel appears in are :
The Death of Baldur.
Ragnarök
Children of Loki
Thor and the Giant's

From Midgard to Hel

Part Five
Burials And Traditions

Different types of burials have been found all over
Europe. Graves that have heavy stone slabs or
stones placed on top of them was believed to stop
the dead from rising. Graves where stones had been
laid out in the shape of a boat where each circle of
stones designates a burial site for a man who had
merit in the community. The well known Mound or
Barrow is where multiple bodies or a body of a
wealthy or important person (Kings or Chieftains)
would be placed. A boat burial is a burial where a
prized boat would be completely buried with its
owner.

Cremations were also another way to send the soul
over to the afterlife. Some cremations took place on
a boat or ship where the body would be cast out
into the water and set on fire. Some cremations took
place where the body would be placed on a cart and
set on fire. Somewhere that had spiritual meaning to
the person was also be used for final goodbyes and
the body would be laid on a pile of logs and set on
fire. After the fire had died the ashes would be
collected and placed in an urn and given to the
persons family or placed in a barrow.

In all these types of burials and cremations,
possessions were placed in with the body to be
taken with them to the afterlife. Boats, horses,
weapons, slaves, clothes, gold/silver, combs and

other things that were seen to be needed in the afterlife were all placed with the body.

In some burials or cremations a Gothi (Spiritual Leader) or matriarch of the village/town would often take charge of the ceremony. It is possible that offerings of food, drink or items of value would often be brought to give to the gods, wights and ancestors at the funeral or local Hof. On the seventh day after the person had died people celebrated the sjaund also called the funeral ale. The funeral ale was a social way of deciding on the inheritance like for example the amount of land given to a certain relative. It was only after this event of drinking the funeral ale that everyone could rightfully claim their inheritance.

A short description on Volva by Nick Wouters

"In some towns they had a Volva, a woman who practises Seidr (a type of sorcery). These women were highly respected but also feared because they had the power to change your Wyrd (fate or personal destiny). They had the power to change what the Norn (female beings that rule the destiny of men and gods) had in store for you. Their way of having this power was of 'magic thought communication' with the ancestors and wights."

Also in the late Viking age there were a few documented manuscripts that mentioned the belief in reincarnation.

Picture By Ben Desmond France 2019

Upon excavations archaeologists have found within some Viking graves small metal amulets that resemble a Mjolnir (the hammer of the god Thor). Mjolnir is recognised as one of the most distinctive religious symbols in the Norse heathen belief. Mjolnir in mythology was known as a main defence against the frost giants but also as a protection of man and gods . Mjolnir is also known for its life giving, in one story Thor and Loki feast upon Thor's goats and after they have finished Thor uses his hammer to bring them back to life.

Thor is one of the sons of Odin, he ruled over features of the atmosphere. Not only just storms but also life giving rain. However its Thor's use of his hammer that protects the world from monsters and giants along with protecting the homes of men and gods. As part of a funeral ceremony for Baldur Thor honours the funeral with Mjolnir. From this action it is known in the belief that Thor's protection continues after death.   I believe that many heathens wear the hammer as protection in life and death because of its symbol of protection .

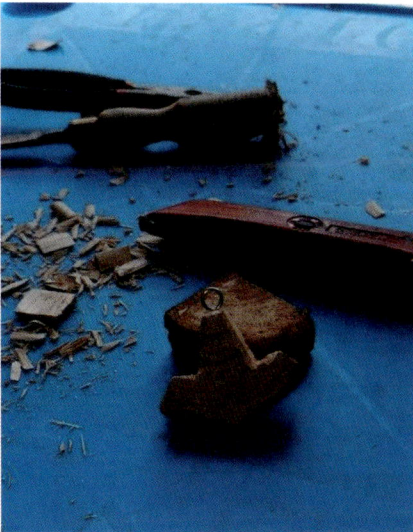

Picture By Ben Desmond France 2019

Thor's Calling

Eyes closed with my head held up high,
    the cold droplets of rain fall upon my face
        as the heavens cry.

The patter of rain drops beat the floor
    like a proud soldier beats his drum of war.
A thrum of thunder
    like clashing of steel upon the battlefield.

In a breath I open my eyes
    to see the storm passing by .

A Poem By Ben Desmond France

Part six
My final words

Picture By Ben Desmond France 2019

I hope I have helped to give you a better understanding into life after death as a Heathen. Although in the end we will rest in Hel or Valhalla/Folkvang (if died as a modern day soldier) I'd still like to think our ancestors who followed other religions would be able to visit us, or us them. From the beginning of my journey in heathenry I have found a strange connection with Hel, a curious one that has kept me wanting to find out more. I have often felt her presence in the shadows at night watching over me and yet I do not fear her There's always a calming/peacefulness about her and the atmosphere when she's around, I presume that's why they say death can be peaceful. Although I have never seen Hel or had her appear in a dream or relaxed spiritual state, the only way I can imagine her appearance is from what I have read in books. I often make offerings to Hel, the Aesir and Vanir at my alter during my home rituals or thanks to the gods and show my respects to Hel. In doing this I hope on my arrival in Hel, the Goddess Hel will save me a comfortable seat at the table, to enjoy a drink with Baldur, my ancestor's and friend's and I hope in my afterlife it will be a relaxing and comfortable one.

Deaths Warning

*The sands of time are slipping away
but far from now will come a day,
There is no time or no warning
when death will come calling.*

*Fate is woven it's out of our hands
when our makers will summon us home,
Be it peacefully or be it harsh
at some point we all must part.*

*Our destination will be unknown
but where we end will be our own,
So take this life and be known
be sure that the right actions are shown.*

A Poem By Ben Desmond France

Extra information & useful links

Thank you for reading my book, if you read this as a non heathen and the heathen belief has took your interest or you want some extra studies/ information, here are a few useful links to community groups in the U.K, pages and websites that may be of use.

Woden Thing Black Country Hearth

Facebook Group & Page (Walsall, West Midlands)

Asatru U.K

www.asatruuk.org

Facebook group /AsatruUk

Twitter/@asatru_uk

The Pagan Federation

www.paganfed.org

The Confederation of UK Heathen Kinreds (for local groups in your area)

Facebook/ ukheathenkinreds

Asgardian Heathen Festival

www.asgardianheathenfestival.co.uk

The Gods' Own County - A Heathen Prayer Book

Facebook/ @thegodsowncounty

UK Heathenry

Facebook Group- UK Heathenry

Heathen Underground

Facebook/ @heathenunderground

Defence Pagan Network

Facebook group/ Defence Pagan Network

From Midgard to Hel

Picture By Ben Desmond France 2019

ABOUT THE AUTHOR

Ben Desmond France

Even though I have dyslexia I've never let it beat me, from that I decided to challenge myself and began writing . A huge influence in my writing is my religion that is Heathenry. Some of my work is based on my family especially my wife and children who inspire me. Friends play a part in my writing as the stories they tell really inspire me to. I have a keen interest in history where I try to visit places of historical connections to topics I am reading in the UK. Not only have I recently been writing poetry but I have just started writing my first fictional book based on a 16-17th century sailor. He gets mixed up between his present world and a Viking world. The book is currently still a work in progress as new content is still being added.

Notes

From Midgard to Hel

Other Work By B.D.France

All From A Dream...

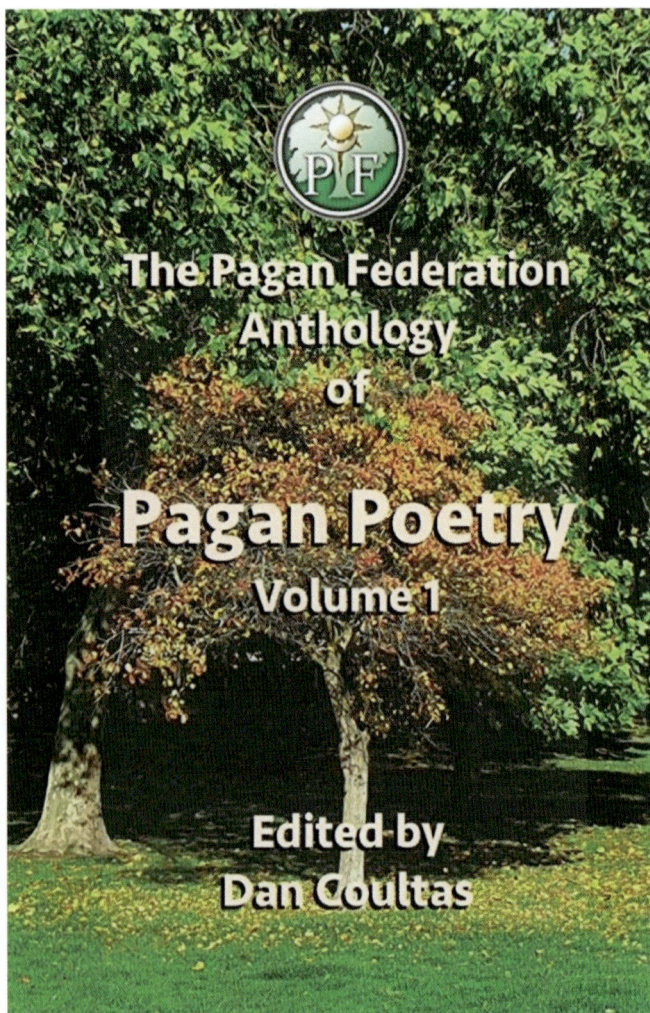

The Pagan Federation
Anthology
of

Pagan Poetry
Volume 1

Edited by
Dan Coultas

From Midgard to Hel

Printed in Great Britain
by Amazon